IMAGES
of America

MITCHELL'S
CORN PALACE

Poem. This poem, taken from an 1893 Corn Belt Exposition souvenir, expressed the ideas of the early builders.

O Mitchell of the Palace grand,
Shall I relate thy story?
Who in mere words can fitly tell
Thy greatness or thy glory?

Thy noble work stands bodily out,
All kindred deeds outvying.
In colors, tints and myriad forms,
Description quite defying.

Thy willing sons and daughters fair,
With interest never lagging,
Have thought and planned with eager brain,
And, wrought with zeal unflagging.

The work of love is now complete;
Each one has done his duty,
Behold thy palace richly crowned—
A Queen of royal beauty!

IMAGES
of America

MITCHELL'S
CORN PALACE

Jan Cerney

ARCADIA
PUBLISHING

Published by Arcadia Publishing
Charleston, South Carolina

Library of Congress Catalog Card Number: 2004100864

For all general information contact Arcadia Publishing at:
Telephone 843-853-2070
Fax 843-853-0044
E-mail sales@arcadiapublishing.com
For customer service and orders:
Toll-Free 1-888-313-2665

Visit us on the Internet at www.arcadiapublishing.com

1992 REPLICA. Clyde Goin and Bob McMahon, grandson of Andrew Kings, the first builder of the original Corn Palace and other Mitchell landmarks, stand by a replica of the first Corn Palace, constructed by Sam Kings.

CONTENTS

ACKNOWLEDGMENTS

I have great admiration for local historical societies and their dedicated members. Their foresight and the selfless hours they spend collecting, storing, and organizing historical documents and photographs safeguard and perpetuate history for succeeding generations to use and enjoy.

I extend special thanks to the Mitchell Area Historical Society and to chairman, Lyle Swenson for suggesting a book on the Corn Palace and for granting me access to the society's archive collection. All the photographs used in this book have been derived from their collection. I am also grateful for Lyle's assistance and for his history knowledge, which has been very helpful to me as I organized the material.

After becoming familiar with the history of the Corn Palace, I gained a growing appreciation for the Corn Palace Committee members' commitment and hard work in staging a new festival every year. I commend the city of Mitchell for the Corn Palace's longevity of over one hundred years.

Thank you to my editor, Samantha Gleisten, and the Arcadia staff for their enthusiasm and guidance and to my family for their support.

The Mitchell Area Historical Society and the author dedicate this book to Clyde Goin, a local historian and Mitchell resident, who has been instrumental in preserving the history of the Corn Palace.

INTRODUCTION

The first Mitchell Corn Palace opened its doors on September 28, 1892, thirteen years after Mitchell was platted. The Mitchell Corn Belt Real Estate Association worked diligently to lure settlers and entrepreneurs to the region. The association watched with interest when the neighboring town of Plankinton and Sioux City, Iowa held harvest festivals housed in grand palace structures decorated in mosaic patterns of corn, grasses, and grain from the agricultural region. Both towns discontinued their expositions within a few years. Representatives of the Corn Belt Real Estate Association traveled to Sioux City to study their plans of the agricultural extravaganza. They liked what they saw and hired Andrew Kings to design a grain-decorated hall for Mitchell to house a harvest festival to be held in the fall to display agriculture products and promote settlement. The association also employed Kansas designer, Alexander Rohe, to add the artistic touches using grains and grasses to decorate the exterior. What resulted was a 60 by 100 foot palace resplendent with magnificent towers and turrets, a shrine to the rural way of life that dominated the scene during the first half of the 20th century.

Trains rumbled into Mitchell during the warm autumn days bringing passengers from across the state to the Corn Belt Exposition. Men in suits and derbies, and women dressed in elegant long dresses and flamboyant hats departed from the trains, whisked the travel dust off their clothing, then took hold of their children's hands and joined the local citizens on the crowded, unpaved streets, bustling with excitement. Shopkeepers stocked their shelves, anticipating extra business and hotel clerks welcomed their patrons. After queuing their way down many blocks from the train to the castle-like structure, the visitors must have certainly been awed by the palace's artistry rendered with natural materials and they looked forward to the live entertainment that would soon appear on the new Corn Palace stage.

The Corn Belt Exposition was so successful that Mitchell expanded the building and held another exposition the following year. The Panic of 1893 and drought halted the exposition for several years until it was revived in 1900. It wasn't until 1902 that the town made an annual commitment to hold the event. The exposition was renamed the Corn Palace Festival in 1905. In that same year, the original wooden building was torn down and replaced with a 125 by 142 foot structure of Moorish design.

For over a hundred years, a magnificent history of entertainment has unfolded at the Corn Palace from the days of vaudeville, variety, and novelty acts, the Big Band Era, television personalities to pop and country music. From the very beginning, the Corn Palace has hosted many great entertainers such as The Thavius Band from Chicago, John Phillips Sousa,

Lawrence Welk and the Hotsy Totsy Boys and Honolulu Fruit Gum Orchestra, Tennessee Ernie Ford, Paul Whiteman, Tommy and Jimmy Dorsey, Harry James, Guy Lombardo, Duke Ellington, Red Skelton, Bob Hope, The Three Stooges, and many others.

The palaces have also staged political events. In 1904, when Mitchell was competing with Pierre for the state capital, one of the most outstanding palaces was erected, a grand display to sway voters to choose Mitchell. In 1908, the Jennings Bryan, William Howard Taft, and Eugene Wilder Chapin political debate drew immense crowds. Twenty years later, Herbert Hoover, then Secretary of Commerce, delivered two addresses to an attentive audience. Gutzon Borglum explained his plans for Mt. Rushmore in 1925. Various political rallies and events have been held since.

The first palaces evoked an international flair, designed with European and Asian motifs and style. Gradually, the artistic style changed to a more Western and South Dakota theme. Colonel Rohe, Dr. Floyd Gillis, Floyd Kings, William Kearny, Oscar Howe, Barbara Young, Don Durfee, Arthur Amiotte, and Cal Schultz used their artistic talents to decorate the Corn Palaces. The third building, built in 1921, still serves as the Corn Palace that we know today and the Corn Palace Committee continues to strive for excellence in entertainment and décor.

The Corn Palace has played a significant role in the economic, cultural, social, political, and historical life of the state. Each Corn Palace has kept to the pulse of the times, weathering the political and economic storms as well as enjoying prosperity. It has endured as a lasting tribute to South Dakota.

CLYDE GOIN. Clyde was appointed Corn Palace Historian by Mayor L.B. "Bud" Williams and served several years in that position. He was also a member of the Corn Palace Committee that oversaw the decoration and operation of the palace. Clyde continues his membership in the Mitchell Area Historical Society.

One

CORN BELT EXPLOSION
1892–1904

1892 CORN PALACE. To further settlement of Mitchell's rich agricultural region, the Mitchell Corn Belt Real Estate Association discussed plans prior to 1892 for a harvest festival event. The idea of a harvest festival extravaganza was not new to the area. The neighboring town of Plankinton housed their festival in a grain-decorated hall a few years earlier. Sioux City, Iowa also constructed palaces to house their exhibits, but abandoned the event after a few years. Lawrence Gale and Louis Beckwith visited Sioux City to learn about constructing a corn palace.

1887 SIOUX CITY CORN PALACE. E.W. Loft, a local architect, drew up a charcoal sketch of the first Sioux City Corn Palace. Between the years 1887 and 1891, five castle-like structures were built. Local women beautifully decorated the interior of the first palace. A mosaic map of the United States, covering one wall, was fashioned from grains and seeds. The focal point was a wax figure of the goddess Ceres posed at the top of a golden stairway of yellow corn.

1888 SIOUX CITY CORN PALACE. The dominant feature of the second Corn Palace was its lofty octagonal tower, which gave the building a fortress-like appearance. Grain covered the entire wooden structure. Inside was a large courtyard surround by display galleries. Three daily concerts entertained the visitors.

10

1889 Sioux City Corn Palace.
A main tower, 200 feet high,
rising over surrounding buildings,
distinguished the third palace.
The 75th New York Regimental
Band performed for visitors
daily. The same year, Sioux City
advertised its Corn Palace with
the Corn Palace Train decorated
like the palaces. A band on board
helped to attract attention as it
traveled the eastern seaboard.

1890 Sioux City Corn Palace. The fourth structure resembled an edifice from the Arabian
Nights. The cupolas and pinnacled towers were similar in design to Islamic mosques. A huge
dome was decorated to look like a globe of the world. Inside the building, designers created a
miniature valley through which a great river flowed. King Korn sat upon a throne.

1891 Sioux City Corn Palace. A horn of plenty spilled out abundant fruit of the harvest from the top of the dome of the final Corn Palace.

1891 Sioux City Corn Palace. The last palace was an enormous, sprawling structure with an arch large enough for traffic to pass through. A popular exhibit was a scene of Romeo and Juliet made from corn silk and husks. The following year, a flood delayed plans for another stunning palace. The flood combined with a financial panic sweeping the nation ended the Sioux City Corn Palace days.

1892 PLANKINTON GRAIN PALACE. Plankinton built the first grain palace in the state in 1891. A sign on the palace read, "Dakota Feeds the World." The palace was built upon a framework of rough lumber, accentuated with towers and gables. A sampling of grains arranged in designs decorated the palace.

1910 GREGORY CORN PALACE. Gregory was designated as one of the registration points in the second Rosebud land opening. The town enlisted the help of Floyd Gillis of Mitchell to construct a grain palace for the event. Ipswich boosters, with the help of J. W. Parmlay, also built a palace in their town in 1907.

1892 MITCHELL CORN PALACE. Gale and Lewis returned home with the idea for a palace decorated with corn, grains, and grasses. The Corn Belt Estate Association accepted the plan and contracted Andrew Kings to erect an arena on the southeast corner of Fourth and Main. The Kansas designer, Alexander Rohe, who had decorated the Sioux City Palace, was hired to design the exterior using native grains and grasses. Mitchell was only thirteen years old with a population of 3,000.

1892 CORN PALACE. The building, constructed with a dirt floor and a seating capacity of 2600, cost $2,976.45. Other expenses incurred were: plumbing $95.27, lighting $264.51, furniture $81.50, decorating $2,248.07, advertising $2,006.51, insurance $59.41, and attractions $2,516.44. The treasurer's report stated that $5,268.67 was raised by contributions and $8,257 from other sources. Sixteen counties agreed to provide agriculture exhibits.

1892 CORN PALACE. The first Corn Palace Committee consisted of L.O. Gale, J.K. Smith, John D. Lawler, Louis Beckwith, T.C. Burns, and N.L. Davison. Beckwith donated the land on which the Corn Palace was built.

1893 CORN PALACE. A 42 by 100 foot addition was built on the north side of the original building. The Lynn Band from Lynn, Massachusetts, the Emmetsburg Band from Emmetsburg, Iowa, and an Indian band cost the committee $3,986. After all the expenses had been paid, the committee had a surplus of over $1,000.

1893 CORN PALACE. Agricultural products commanded the visitor's attention. Monster pumpkins, enormous squashes, beets, turnips, and other bounty of the fields were displayed. Twenty-three varieties of wheat, rye, flax, black barley, white barley, hulled barley, buckwheat, ten varieties of oats, millet, Hungarian clover white and red sunflower seed, alfalfa, and alsike affirmed the productivity of the land. Old King Korn was the reigning product.

1900 CORN PALACE. After the Corn Belt Exposition had been cancelled for six years due to the Panic of 1893 and severe droughts, the festival was revived in 1900. An American eagle became the featured design. The upper floor of the building displayed art. All decorations were crafted from corn, cornhusks, and other varied agricultural products.

1900 CORN PALACE. The electric light company put 75 incandescent lights on the stage and 400 lights throughout the upper and lower floors. Phinney's United States Band of Chicago played to 2,000 attendees.

1902 CORN PALACE. The exposition skipped a year and opened the next with cold rainy weather. The exposition featured juggling, balancing acts, and dancers. Professor DeBaugh and his Twentieth Century Band from Chicago entertained audiences. The Mitchell paper reported, "Fifty cowboys came in off the range with their horses and gave an exciting parade at the close of the afternoon. They rode breakneck speed through Main Street."

17

1903 CORN PALACE. A special ceremony of placing the first stone for the new city hall was part of the opening day of the Corn Belt Exposition. Mitchell was hopeful that the city would win the bid for the state capital the following year. The new courthouse would be able to

accommodate a state government. Banda Rossa, Third Regiment Band of Woonsocket, The Parker Band, and daily street attractions entertained the audiences. Governor Herreid attended the ceremonies and spoke on taxation and assessment.

1903 CORN PALACE INTERIOR. Rows of wooden chairs filled the auditorium area and booths featuring agriculture produce lined the walls. The names of various counties that sponsored each display were written above the booths.

1903 CROWD SCENE. An unidentified man and a child enjoy the festivities along with a large crowd. The Corn Belt Exposition was such a popular event that Sioux City expressed regret for letting Mitchell borrow their idea.

1903 CORN PALACE.
The Third Regiment
Band of Woonsocket
marches in front of the
Corn Palace.

1904 CORN PALACE. Mitchell made a bid for the state capital title in 1904. The Corn Belt Committee went all out that year feeling that the Corn Palace would be an asset, especially with the engagement of John Phillips Sousa and his band. Even though the palace was considered the most beautiful of all, decorated in Navajo motifs surrounded by Grecian borders, Pierre won the bid for the government seat. The mayor gave notice that the throwing and use of rubber balls and confetti were prohibited.

OFFICIAL PROGRAMME
Corn Belt Exposition
Mitchell, South Dakota

THURSDAY AFTERNOON, SEPT. 29, 1904

For Comfort and Pleasure of All, Ladies are Requested to Remove their Hats

Grand Concert by Sousa and his Band
JOHN PHILIP SOUSA, Conductor

ESTELLE LIEBLING, Soprano.
LEO ZIMMERMAN, Trombone
HERBERT L. CLARKE, Cornet

1904 PROGRAM. The official program of the Corn Belt Exposition advertised the Grand Concert by Sousa and his band. To Sousa's astonishment, Mitchell agreed to pay him and his band $7,000 a day for six days. Disillusioned when he arrived and saw the small prairie town surround with mud-filled streets, he refused to leave the train without the money in hand. Notice was also given on the program that "For the comfort and pleasure of all, ladies are required to remove their hats."

Two

CORN PALACE FESTIVAL
1905–1920

1905 CORN PALACE. A new Corn Palace building was erected on its new site, the northeast corner of Fifth and Main, 55 days after laying the first corner stone. The Corn Belt Exposition now became know as the Corn Palace Festival. At the new palace, the Italian Band, Rossa performed the "Resurrection of Christ" to a packed house. Nine train coaches, loaded to the brim with passengers, came to Mitchell on a Saturday afternoon.

1905 MAIN STREET. Mitchell's Main Street was a crowded affair during the Corn Palace festivities. The Corn Palace can be seen in the background.

1905 CORN PALACE. Dr. Dundas, a Corn Palace committee member, promised that he could have the new building up and running in no time. In less than two months, it was completed.

1905 FESTIVAL ATTENDEES. Mr. and Mrs. Milton Dowdell, prominent Mitchell citizens, chat in front of the Corn Palace while an unidentified man looks on. The Dowdells were related to Israel and Herman Greene, early surveyors around Firesteel. Israel also fought in the Civil War.

1906 CORN PALACE. It took approximately 1,500 bushels of corn to decorate the Corn Palace. Each year, Colonel Rohe of Lawrence, Kansas came to Mitchell to transform the palace into magnificent displays featuring intense geometric designs. The theme was "The Kilties are Coming." The Kilties were billed as the world's greatest Scotch band.

1906 CROWD SCENE. The Corn Palace Festival lost money this year because of the newly built Gale Theater, one of the finest in the state. The theater offered competing programs to the crowds pouring in off the trains. Horse racing also edged out the income.

1907 CORN PALACE. The symbol prominent in the foreground, now known to us as representing the Swastika of the Third Reich, has drawn confusion and anger over the years. The symbol dates back thousands of years and represents prosperity, peace, and good fortune. It was used in innocence as simply an Indian peace sign, visually appealing to the eye at that time.

1907 SOUSA'S BAND. Sousa returned to the palace for another engagement. He had discovered on his last trip in 1904 that the Corn Palace was enchanting and the crowds enthusiastic.

1908 CORN PALACE. Thavius Band from Chicago was the main attraction in addition to political visits from Bryan, Taft, and Chapin. Other entertainment included vaudeville programs, foot juggling, comedy, music, mimics, acrobatics, and strongman acts. In the *Mitchell Clarion*, the Lyon Novelty Company advertised a free Ingersoll watch to any boy and girl who could sell 30 colored postcards of the Corn Palace at ten cents each. Dr. Floyd Gillis, former assistant to Colonel Rohe, took over decorating responsibilities.

1908 BRYAN'S VISIT. William Jennings Bryan visited the Corn Palace to campaign for his Democratic candidacy for president. He is not specifically identified in the photo.

1908 TAFT'S VISIT. Republican William Howard Taft, standing in the automobile, was then Secretary of War as he campaigned for the presidency in Mitchell. The third candidate, Eugene Wilder Chapin, representing the Prohibition Party, also campaigned but is not pictured.

1909 Corn Palace. Moorish designed minarets, turrets, and kiosks dominated the elegantly designed palace. The United States Marine Band headlined the entertainment. The Milwaukee Railroad ran special trains to keep up with the throngs of people wishing to attend. Rates were reported to be so low that it was cheaper to attend the Corn Palace than to stay home.

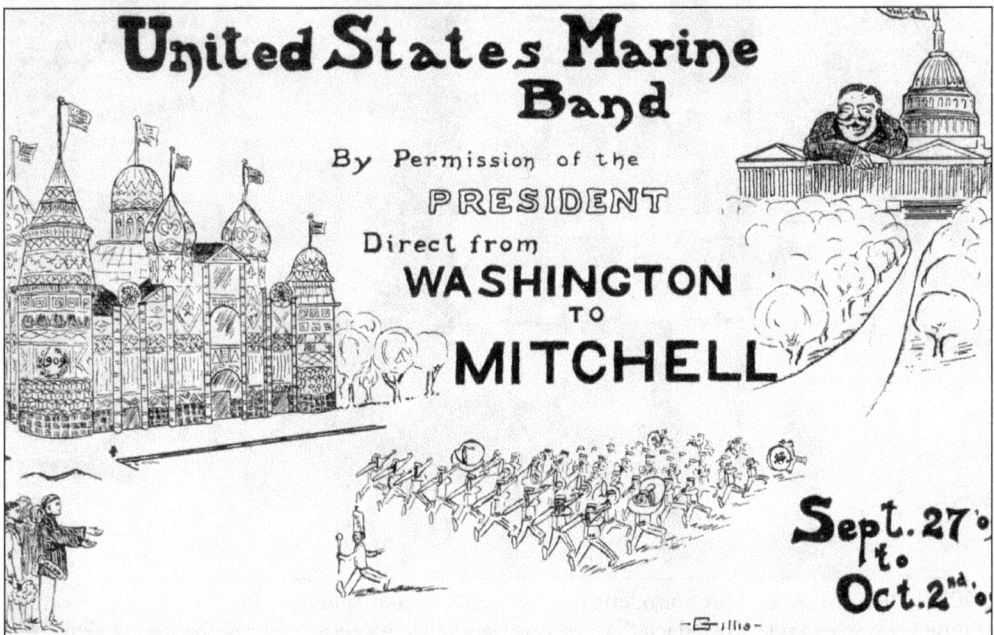

1909 Postcard. A postcard advertised the United States Marine Band as the main attraction for the 1909 Corn Palace. The smiling president was none other than William Howard Taft.

1909 U.S. MARINE BAND. The U.S. Marine Band stands in front of the intricately designed Corn Palace. "The Marine Band is recognized all over the country and beyond as the best-conducted and strongest musical attraction in existence," quoted a Mitchell newspaper.

1909 CORN PALACE. Three unidentified gentlemen take time out for a picture in front of the newly decorated Corn Palace. The strong geometric patterns give the photo an old world flavor. Twenty-year old Floyd Gillis, a Davison County native, who had taken over the work of decorating the palace, began the practice of showing scenes from South Dakota.

1910 CORN PALACE. Nine counties were represented in agriculture exhibits. The exhibits gave the farmers a chance to display their prize crops and gain ideas from others. Prizes were awarded for best displays. The Corn Palace, decorated in Indian designs, hosted Pat Conway's Band.

1910 CONWAY'S BAND. Conway's 45-piece band posed in front of Indian designs skillfully crafted from colored corn, other grains, and grasses. The DeMont trio of acrobats also entertained audiences. Free street acts were also a popular feature of the festivities.

1912 Corn Palace. A $10,000 European hippodrome was the main attraction. Forty men and boys were employed to decorate the lavish palace at a cost of more than $5,000. Since the fire danger was always imminent in or near the building, a horse-drawn cart with a reel of hose was stationed by the hydrant on the corner of the building. No smoking was allowed.

1912 Souvenir Postcard. Corn Palace visitors posed in an imitation hot-air balloon for their souvenir snapshot commemorating their festival visit.

1913 CORN PALACE. By 1913, decorations were swinging towards central themes. This Corn Palace displayed a western motif. The streets were paved in concrete and wooden light poles were replaced with metal poles displaying clustered light fixtures. A circus with a live band was the main attraction. Farmers had produced the best harvest in years. Receipts and attendance exceeded all prior years.

1911 CORN PALACE. 1911 was a turning point for the Corn Palace's artistic design. Geometric designs of the past were giving way to other motifs. An Egyptian design predominated. This

was also the first year a new building operated without debt payment. However, little confetti was thrown in celebration.

1913 PARADE. The parade down the newly paved streets reflected the western theme of the newly decorated Corn Palace. Street vendors were allowed to sell food for the first time.

1914 CORN PALACE. Performers included Francesco Ferullo, vaudeville acts, and circus acrobats. The Tripp County Band, a high wire artist and Rollo the Limit, doing "loop the loop" on roller skates were among the free street attractions. The theme was centered on a Dutch motif.

ENTERTAINER. No date is given for this photograph of Mary Aples. She skated with the Skating McGowans when they performed at the Corn Palace.

1915 CORN PALACE. Ferrullo's Band performed for the second consecutive year. Other features were a stage aeroplane act, women acrobats and a bicycle troupe.

1915 QUEEN. Dakota Wesleyan University senior Helen Goss was crowned queen of the Corn Palace. Her royal court and a band stand in the background next to her conveyance were decorated in corn and cornhusks.

1916 CORN PALACE. Below normal temperatures and the appearance of Charlie Chaplin at the Gale Theater hindered attendance. The Liberati Band, organized in 1889, played to audiences. World War I was still raging in Europe during 1916. With war on the minds of everyone, the palace decorated in a patriotic theme.

1917 CORN PALACE. Fairly large crowds attended despite the lack of train service and bad roads. Because of U.S. involvement in the war, a patriotic theme predominated. Vaudeville acts appeared at the palace along with the Great Innis. An elaborate automobile parade awed the spectators. The 50-piece Great Innis Band struck up the "Star Spangled Banner" on soldier's night, honoring the soldiers who fought in the Great War.

1918 CORN PALACE. Signs of war were visible at the palace. Flyers given out on street corners urged people to buy war bonds. The main attraction was the Liberty Train pulling dozens of cars loaded with war relics. Great Innis Five Star Band performed for another year.

1919 CORN PALACE. A carnival atmosphere pervaded the palace. The war was over. The visitors threw confetti and paper streamers and blew horns. Col. Theodore Roosevelt Jr. made an appearance. The Corn Palace was held in a tent in 1920 as the old building was torn down and the new building was not ready.

Three

A NEW CORN PALACE
1921–1936

1921 CORN PALACE. A new Corn Palace building was erected on the corner of Sixth and Main at a cost of $200,000. It doubled the seating capacity of the old structure to 5,000. No longer was the entire building covered in corn and grains. Decorated panels were used on the outside depicting the year's theme. The Karl King Band entertained the audiences.

1922 CORN PALACE. A grillwork of grasses and grains around the top of the structure and raising the flagpole gave an illusion of height to the building, distracting from the otherwise square appearance. The nation's coal strike was settled when Corn Palace decorating was under way. The five-month strike caused lapses in rail transportation and depressed the livestock market.

1923 CORN PALACE. Ernie Young presented a sensational review. The highlight of the show was Young's Golden Girls. Four Hundred dollars worth of pearls covered each of the girl's costumes. Attempts were made to steal the costumes, and an extra guard was posted. Two of the costumes were stolen anyway. "Big Jim," an Alaskan bear, trained to wrestle with a man entertained the audiences.

1924 CORN PALACE. Clarice Catlett was the prima donna of the festival. Three of the panels were designed in classical themes of Italian, Egyptian, and oriental motifs. Other panels portrayed an eagle astride two great horns of plenty and scenes from the West.

1924 MINIATURE CORN PALACE. A truck transports a replica of the Corn Palace to the parade.

1925 CORN PALACE. Gutzon Borglum revealed his plans for Mt. Rushmore during the Corn Palace. South Dakota Governor Carl Gunderson and Senators Peter Norbeck and W.M. McMaster accompanied him. John Phillips Sousa played the Corn Palace that year but not during Corn Palace week. This was his third appearance.

1926 CORN PALACE. Designers used a new grain, Chinese buckwheat, for the first time. David Flanigan, nationally known trick and fancy rifle shooting artist, and Ed and Mae, America's top gymnasts, made their appearances. U.S. Secretary of Commerce Herbert Hoover delivered a speech to community leaders. A Charleston dance contest topped off the entertainment.

44

1926 DANCER. Jane Smith, a ballet dancer, made her appearance in "Stepping Out."

1927 CORN PALACE. An array of vaudeville stars took to the stage and entertained audiences who paid one dollar apiece for admission. The murals donned scenes of vaudeville.

1928 CORN PALACE. Miss Universe, Ella Van Husen of Chicago, made a big hit at the festival. The decorations were veiled due to rain. After the final touches were completed, they, then, were uncovered.

1929 Corn Palace. The Campus Cuties, 25 young dancing women, entertained crowds with their sensational production. A want ad in the paper called for all Mitchell's youth to dress in traditional pioneer garb. All costumes were judged.

1929 ENTERTAINERS. Fourteen members of the Bricktops, an all-girl song and dance show, bedazzled audiences.

1930 CORN PALACE. The region was experiencing drought conditions. Newspaper headlines read that the town was "dry" but not due to drought but to law enforcement working diligently to keep alcohol off the streets. Twelve varieties of corn were displayed. Eleven counties were represented with exhibits.

1931 CORN PALACE. The orchestra leader, Benny Meroff, headlined the palace. It took a special baggage car to bring the orchestra's 37 trunks and 155 musical instruments to Mitchell. The year's celebration was designed to make everyone forget the drought and Great Depression. Because of the drought, a wide variety of colored corn was difficult to obtain.

1931 BENNY MEROFF. The yearly program described Benny Meroff as "America's most versatile orchestra leader. He is a combination singer, dancer, musician and comedian, four talents rarely assembled in one man. He plays fifteen different instruments."

1931 ENTERTAINERS. Cato's Vagabonds performed at the Corn Palace during the year. Periodically, special entertainment would be booked throughout the year to coincide with other events.

ENTERTAINER. The unidentified entertainer and many like her brought glamour and elegance to the Corn Palace stage.

OFFICIAL PROGRAM

World's Only

Corn Palace

Mitchell, U. S. A.

SEPT. 28 - OCT. 3

1931

King Korn's
Autumn
Festival

DOORS OPEN 1 P. M. AND
7 P. M.
CURTAIN 2 P. M., 8 P. M.

(Keep Your Program for a
Souvenir—Read the Ads)

1931 PROGRAM. The year's official program included these encouraging words, "This printed program has been given you that you may more easily follow the progress of the show. It is given with the compliments of the Mitchell and other South Dakota business firms which carry advertising...They want you to forget your troubles and be with them in their optimistic look ahead, as indicated in the theme of the revue—'Hello Prosperity.' "

1932 CORN PALACE. The Radio-Keith Orpheum Vaudeville Troupe entertained with their comedy and singing. Political speaker Mrs. Dolly Gann spoke in behalf of her brother, Vice President Curtis Hoover. Ruth Bryan Owen discussed the Democratic platform.

1933 PANEL. The decorating committee found itself without funds to decorate the Corn Palace as the money was tied up in a closed bank. The Kiwanis Club, at the suggestion of its member Milton Dowdell, offered to decorate a panel. Other service clubs participated in decorating the palace also.

1933 CORN PALACE. Lou Breese and his band headlined at the palace. Comedian Eddie Russell and magician Lou Semb, presenting an illusion of a woman burning alive, rounded out the performances.

1934 CORN PALACE. Forty thousand people attended the palace. Over two inches of welcome rain opened the festival. Frankie Masters and his band were the main attraction.

1934 FRANKIE MASTERS. The Corn Palace program introduced Masters with these words. "Frankie Masters and his orchestra need no introduction to the thousands of radio fans who have been thrilled by their music for many months. Frankie is not only a director of high merit, but a composer, singer, producer and a lot of other things that Corn Palace visitors like."

1935 CORN PALACE. Sets of twins from all over the states were invited to be guests of a twin sister singing act, The Hilton Sisters. Unfortunately the Hilton Sisters broke their singing engagement due to illness but twins from around the country attended anyway. Herbie Kay and his orchestra entertained.

1935 FARMERS' DAY. The Corn Palace also hosted other events such as Farmers' Day held in February.

1936 CORN PALACE. Bernie Cummins and his orchestra, vaudeville acts, and Janet Reed—the "Darling of the Toe Dance," were among the performers. Col. Frank Knox, Republican nominee for vice president, made the Corn Palace part of his campaign swing.

Four

BIG BAND ERA
1937–1959

1937 CORN PALACE. The palace was remodeled by adding minarets, turrets, and kiosks of Moorish design. The Turkish mosques and minarets were worked out in designs and the panels were decorated with scenes using the usual corn and grains. Isham Jones and his world famous 17-piece band performed.

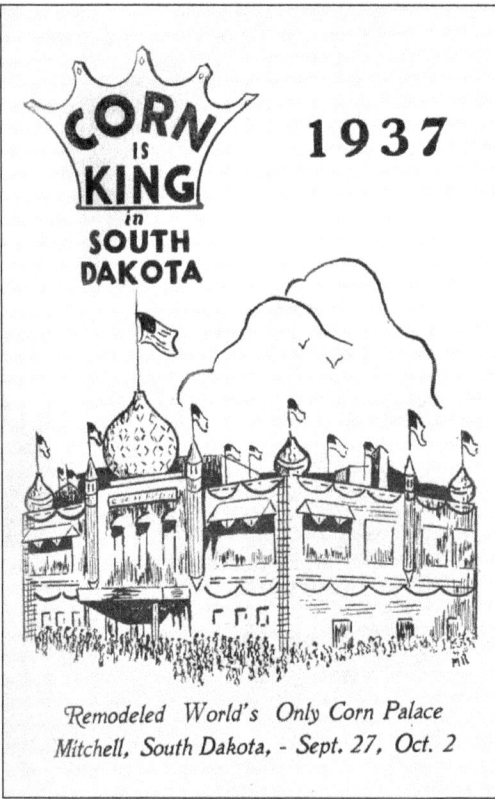

1937 PROGRAM. The program informed the crowds of midway entertainment. "When you leave the Corn Palace after the grand finale of the 1937 show, you will go out into the midway filled with attractions, which will help make this a real holiday occasion."

1937 PANEL. The halved ears of corn are very visible in this desert scene.

1937 PANEL. For the first time in four years, there was enough corn available to complete all decorations.

1938 CORN PALACE. The new, modern palace featured a streamlined design. It was decorated with living trees as well as normal grain designs. The Forest Service exhibited trees in hopes that farmers and other landowners would plant shelterbelts around their property. Jimmy Dorsey was the headline attraction.

1939 CORN PALACE. The price of general admission was six bits. Anyone who had lived in Mitchell for the past 50 years was admitted free. Paul Whitman and his Chesterfield Orchestra provided the main entertainment.

1939 PANEL. A mural depicts the family farm. The decade of the 1930s was very trying for the farmer and as a result many had to leave their beloved farms.

1939 PANEL. A mural was designed for Paul Whiteman, "The King of Jazz," a title he gave himself. Whiteman's orchestra was the most popular band in the 1920s and was known for its signature tune, Gershwin's "Rhapsody in Blue." Among all his accomplishments, Whiteman is credited with discovering Bing Crosby.

1940 CORN PALACE. The theme for the year was "America First." Panels were designed showing Uncle Sam's disdain toward Communism. The south side of the palace displayed insignias of the United States Army and Navy, Marine Corps, and American Red Cross. Johnny "Scat" Davis and his orchestra were the main attraction.

1941 CORN PALACE. William Kerney designed panels featuring sportsmen enjoying the fall hunting season. New lights illuminated the panels after dark. "Stars over America" revue produced by Ernie Young provided entertainment. Norma Ballard, "Lady of 1,001 Songs," opened each performance. This was the first time in history that decorations were unveiled in advance of the festival to permit tourists to view them.

1942 CORN PALACE. Gary Gordon and his orchestra performed for the audiences who came to celebrate the theme "Victory". Murals depicted the allied powers attacking the enemy. Red, white, and blue carried out the patriotic theme.

1943 CORN PALACE. Thoughts of the war overshadowed the festival. "Take Time for Happiness" was the theme. WAVE, WAC, Army and Navy recruiting exhibits were on display as well as Joe Foss's trophies. South Dakota's Foss made a mark in the war as a fighter pilot. Russ Morgan and his orchestra provided music for dancing every night at the conclusion of the show.

1943 MORGAN. Russ Morgan signed his portrait with these words. "To the Corn Palace Committee from a 'Brother Corn Cribber' —We entertainers and musicians are <u>not</u> always treated as nice as you treated us—so—for everybody Thanks Russ Morgan."

63

1943 MIDWAY. The Corn Palace midway was known as the Northwest's largest midway.

1944 CORN PALACE. Due to lack of grain and manpower because of the war, decorating tradition was set aside. The murals were painted. Glen Gray and his Casa Loma Band were the featured entertainers. The midway was seven blocks long with 78 rides.

1944 PROGRAM. A page from the program highlights the entertainment of Elno Tanner, "World's Greatest Whistler" and Gilbert and Lee, "The Howl of the Year."

1945 CORN PALACE. Red and yellow corn spelled out the theme "Victory and Peace." Ten thousand pounds of corn as well as milo, cane, millet, and oats were used in decorating. Four carnivals and numerous independent showmen appeared on the midway. Frankie Carle Orchestra was the featured entertainment.

1946 CORN PALACE. The palace received a new look after the war. An improved $4,000 lighting system was installed. The theme "America the Beautiful" was reflected in 12 scenes of South Dakota's wildlife and native America. Ray McKinley's orchestra, a favorite of the GI's, provided entertainment along with the Dining Sisters, Bert Wheeler, and Borah Mennovitch and his Harmonies Rascals.

1947 CORN PALACE. Tommy Dorsey headlined the show. A reporter wrote, "In the large crowd that greeted him were a number of bobby-soxers." Three carnivals provided entertainment on the midway. Eight bands from various South Dakota towns gave concerts each day. Harold Strassen, Republican candidate for president, spoke. Mayor Hubert Humphrey of Minneapolis, Minnesota, represented the Democratic Party.

1947 PANEL. The close up of the mural advertised the Corn Palace as being, "The Midwest's Greatest Show."

1948 CORN PALACE. Victor Borge, "Crown Prince of Keyboard," and Lawrence Welk were the headliners. During one performance, some loose grain fell on the stage startling musicians and dancers so that they stopped performing. "It's just corn," said the North Dakota-raised Lawrence Welk.

1948 PANEL. Oscar Howe, a local artist, became the new Corn Palace designer. Howe was born on the Crow Creek Reservation in 1915, descending from a line of Yanktonnais chiefs. He learned to draw Indian symbols from his grandmother early in life. After boarding school, he attended the Santa Fe Indian School where his talent in art flourished.

1948 LAWRENCE WELK.
Lawrence Welk would make many appearances at the Corn Palace during his career. He began in the 1930s as a traveling musician, accordion player, and bandleader, specializing in dance tunes.

1949 CORN PALACE. Skitch Henderson and his orchestra with Bob Crosby as master of ceremonies, performed along with other entertainers: Comedian Johnny Morgan, English ventriloquist Clifford Guest, Monica Lewis and five Broadway acts. Newspapers reported a surprising number of visitors from Nebraska, Iowa, and Minnesota.

1949 PANEL. Oscar Howe's handiwork depicts a farmer and a Native American giving thanks. Howe learned to paint murals while studying at the Indian Art Center in Lawton, Oklahoma. Prior to that, the WPA hired him to paint scenes on the domed ceiling of the Mitchell Library. Mobridge hired him to do ten historical murals for the town's new auditorium.

1949 PANEL. Oscar Howe decorated and produced a complete new series of Indian and early Dakota pictures.

1950 CORN PALACE. Harry James and his orchestra played to the first sell-out crowd in history. Harry James' wife, Betty Grable, caused quite a stir when she arrived. Because of her contract with Twentieth Century Fox, she could not set foot on the Corn Palace stage. She said that she enjoyed South Dakota's clean air and commented on the rich-looking farm soil.

1951 CORN PALACE. The Horace Heidt Youth Opportunity Program constituted the show. Decorations depicted the history of South Dakota from the time of Indians to scenes of present day agriculture, industry, and transportation.

1952 CORN PALACE. Broadcast nationally, Guy Lombardo and his Royal Canadians played to record crowds. Designs represented major holidays celebrated in South Dakota style. The first frost of the season drove flies indoors where they pestered entertainers and the audience as well.

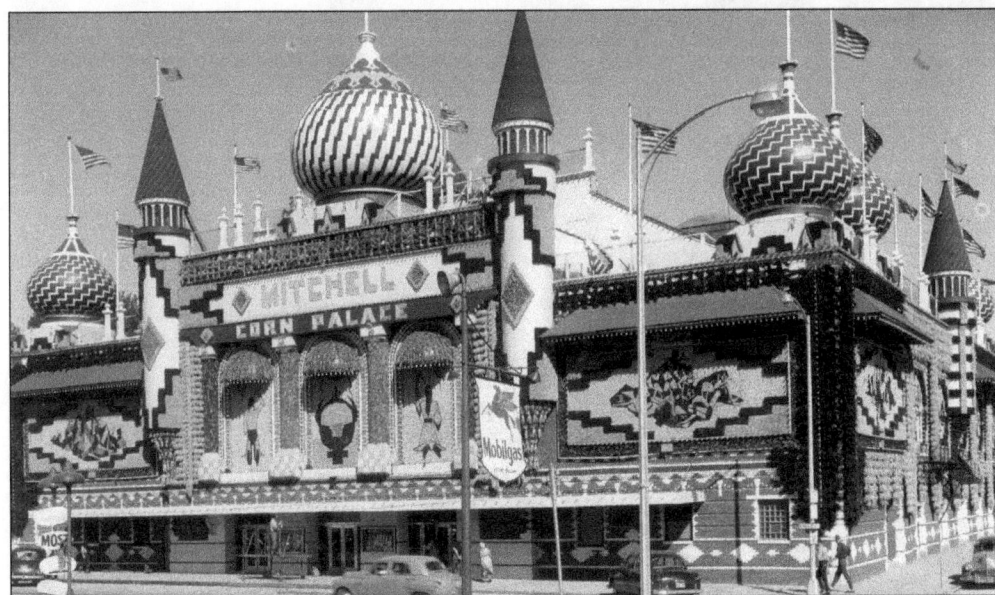

1953 CORN PALACE. Duke Ellington and his orchestra shared the spotlight with Judy Canova. Other entertainment included a twirling duo of Ted and Flo Ballett, the singing group, Pretty Girls in the Woods, the Lancasters performing aerobic stunts, and the trampoline act of the All American Boys.

1954 CORN PALACE. Ominous skies threatened the Corn Palace as the Lawrence Welk show shattered attendance records. It was reported that Welk earned $29,746.80. Hamm's Northernaires, a nationally known drum and bugle corps, also appeared. Howe selected an all South Dakota theme.

1954 MYRON FLOREN. Floren was the featured accordionist for Lawrence Welk and his Champagne Music Show. Floren would make many more appearances at the Corn Palace.

1955 CORN PALACE. The warm, muggy weather greeted headliner Freddie Martin along with thousands of bugs invading the palace. Other entertainers included an Egyptian acrobat team, Bud and Cece Robinson, the King Sisters, and Betty and Benny Fox.

1955 PANEL. This was the eighth year that Oscar Howe created designs. He focused on wildlife as the central theme. After graduation from Dakota Wesleyan in 1952, he began work on a Master of Fine Arts degree at the University of Oklahoma. He then became an art director at the Pierre public school system. In the meantime, he won many prizes for his work.

1955 ENTERTAINERS. Bud and Cece autographed their picture with these words. "To the Corn Palace Committee—Thanks for having us! It was a big thrill and we loved every minute in Mitchell."

1956 CORN PALACE. Panels portrayed ox-drawn wagons and settlers, the Mitchell-Pierre Capital fight, pioneer churches, old Corn Palaces, and the first wood burning engine pulling into Mitchell.

1956 CORN PALACE. Patti Page and Tony Pastor and his band delighted the audiences. Howe designed a replica of history beginning with the Arikara Indians to the present, illuminated here with the evening lights.

1956 Tony Pastor. In the 1930s, Pastor joined Artie Shaw's band and became one of its featured soloists. He then tried band leading and became successful after a series of radio broadcasts. He hired Betty and Rosemary Clooney to sing along with his band. He continued as bandleader until the end of the 1950s. Some of his known songs were "Bell Bottom Trousers," "Please Don't Squeeze De Banana," and "Dance With the Dolly."

1957 Corn Palace. Fifteen thousand dollars was spent for decorations featuring a sport's motif. Ray Anthony, "The Young Man With the Horn," entertained audiences.

1958 GUY LOMBARDO. Lombardo started as an orchestra leader with members of his family in his hometown of London, Ontario. Lombardo and his ensemble, The Royal Canadians, sold at least 100 million records, topping the charts between 1929 and 1952.

1958 CORN PALACE. Guy Lombardo headlined at the palace. Modes of transportation used throughout the area from days of the Indians to the present decorated the panels. Mr. Allen, an 83 year old area resident, delivered a load of corn to the palace with a team and wagon. He had provided white decorating corn for the past 54 years.

1959 CORN PALACE. A drought hurt the availability of red corn for decorating. Howe designed scenes typical of the Middle Border. Included were a pair of trappers and an Indian women welcoming a riverboat. Crowds enjoyed Shep Fields and his orchestra, the Manhattan Rockets, Snooky Lanson, Elkins Sisters, and the Mills Brothers.

Five

SOUTH DAKOTA THEMES
1960–1979

1960 CORN PALACE. The Lennon Sisters headlined the show. Other entertainers included Jimmy Dean, Buddy Morrow and Night Train Orchestra, Jo Ann Castle and her honky-tonk player piano, Roger Ray, Zippy the Chimpanzee, the Manhattan Chorus Line, and Trio Baranton—foot juggler. Oscar Howe designed the theme around communications. The panels portrayed scenes of smoke signals, the pony express, telegraph, telephone, and others.

1960 JO ANN CASTLE. Castle, a member of the Lawrence Welk show, was reported to have won "the biggest hand of the evening" in applause. She signed on as a regular of the Welk show in 1959.

PANEL. Created from split ears of corn, this interior panel depicts the earliest days of South Dakota history.

1961 CORN PALACE. As usual, the Corn Palace offered quality entertainment with the Three Stooges, Pee Wee Hunt, Peter Palmer Voices and Orchestra, the Manhattan Rockets, Lotti Brun—female juggler, and the Six Staneks, performing acrobatics. "Dakota Territory" was the theme of the beautiful palace décor.

1961 PETER PALMER. Peter Palmer conducted his own band through college before becoming a professional bandleader. He added voices and choir to his orchestra as a mark of distinction.

1962 CORN PALACE. Lawrence Welk headlined the show once more. The theme "South Dakota, Yesterday and Today" was reflected in seven panels displaying scenes such as the origin of corn, a deer silhouetted in front of Mt. Rushmore, a pheasant in flight, and a cowboy roping a wild horse.

1962 PANEL. The interior panel made entirely of split ears of corn portrays the magnificent Mt. Rushmore Monument.

The Lennon Sisters
ATURED WITH LAWRENCE WELK
Lucky & Luck
HOLLYWOOD · NEW YORK

1962 LENNON SISTERS. The Lennon Sisters appeared regularly with the televised Lawrence Welk Show. Pictured are Kathy, Diane, and Peggy.

1963 HOWE AND WELK. Oscar Howe points to his artistic rendition of Lawrence Welk's likeness. Welk seems to approve. By the 1960s, Howe was well-established and very successful in the art world. In 1960, Governor Herseth appointed Howe as the South Dakota Artist Laureate. He was the recipient of many awards and honors well into the 1970s.

1963 CORN PALACE. Crowds pack the palace to see Lawrence Welk and his "Champagne Music" makers. He appeared at 15 sell-out performances. The Lawrence Welk Show first appeared on television in 1955 and lasted for 27 years.

1963 HOWE, WELK, AND EPPEL. Oscar Howe, Lawrence Welk, and Ray Eppel take time out from their busy schedules for a picture. Ray was a Corn Palace Committee member and owner of KORN radio and television.

DECORATING A PANEL. Various farmers in the area specialize in growing white, red, blue, and shades of yellow corn for decorating the Corn Palace. Other farmers contract for a given amount of grain such as oats, milo, sudan grass, barley, and other grains. The artist develops and paints miniature panels and then lays out each panel in full scale in chalk on black roofing paper. The artist marks what color is to cover a given section. Using the aid of scaffolding, the workers tack the roofing paper to the large panel. Decorators tie grasses and grains in bunches to use as trim according to the design which they put in place before the panels are created. They use power equipment to saw individual ears of corn in half lengthwise. The halved corn is then nailed flat side to the panel.

88

1963 PANEL. Colorful wildlife scenes of waterfowl, hunting pheasants, a dog chasing a raccoon up a tree, and other displays decorated the palace. Time, weather, pigeons, and squirrels take their toll on the decorative panels. A repellent and preservative are applied to maintain the life of the corn and grains a little longer.

1963 WELK DANCING. Lawrence Welk surprised residents of Brady Memorial Home. He is pictured dancing with an unidentified lady. Myron Floren is playing the accordion.

1964 CORN PALACE. The palace featured Andy Williams along with the Osmond Brothers. The palace murals depicted South Dakota scenes of a riding club, a rancher and his cattle, and a sheepherder and his sheep.

1964 ANDY WILLIAMS. Williams began entertaining at age nine when he and his three brothers, Don, Bob, and Dick, worked up an act and appeared on a radio show in Des Moines, Iowa. Although Andy Williams admitted that he almost gave up his pursuit, he managed to persevere and eventually achieved fame.

1964 OSMONDS. The Osmond Brothers began their career with appearances on The Andy Williams Show. Pictured are Jay, Merrill, Wayne, and Alan. Donnie, not pictured, was six then and was occasionally worked into the show. The brothers were described as "well behaved, sparkling personalities."

1965 CORN PALACE. Brenda Lee appeared in the newly remodeled Corn Palace. The project cost $800,000, but the palace would now include a new basketball court, color- coded seating sections, and a 70-foot stage. Basketball games would accommodate 4,000 fans.

1966 MIDWAY. The unidentified Corn Palace attendees enjoy the Ferris wheel, one of the many attractions on the midway.

1966 CORN PALACE. A drought caused another corn shortage. Two decorative panels were eliminated and the size of the others was reduced. "Reminders of the Past" was the theme. Tennessee Ernie Ford inspired the audiences.

1966 TENNESSEE ERNIE FORD. Ford, the "pea picker" from Tennessee, was known for his folksy ways and down home music which often included gospels, hymns, and spirituals. He hosted a top-rated television series from 1956-1965 and closed each show with a hymn.

1967 CORN PALACE. Jack Benny, a veteran of 55 years in show business, Bobby Vinton know for his "Blue Velvet," Skitch Henderson, and Mary Lou Collins, whose voice was compared to Barbara Streisand, performed to audiences. Ten area bands played on the midway.

1967 PANEL. Workers follow the instructions on the black roofing paper to create the mural of the playing band displayed on the 1967 Corn Palace.

1968 CORN PALACE. The Golddiggers, from Dean Martin's summer show fame, opened the Corn Palace. Eddie Arnold sang to appreciative audiences. Arnold commented that the Corn Palace was just as professional as any other theater that he had played in New York City.

1969 CORN PALACE. The Lawrence Welk show filled the house. The demand for tickets was so high that box office hours were extended to meet the demand. Welk surprised audiences, appearing on stage with long hair and a vest. "I'm doing the now thing," he told them. He then disappeared backstage and reappeared with short hair and his usual impeccable attire. A space age theme decorated the palace.

1970 CORN PALACE. Tennessee Ernie Ford headlined once again. Other entertainers included The Brothers and Sisters, Comedian Glen Ash, and Ford's orchestra arranger and leader Jack Fascinato. The Murphy's Show provided midway entertainment.

1971 CORN PALACE. Andy Griffith, Jerry Van Dyke, and a young singing group known as The Establishment entertained audiences. Governor Kneip commended Mitchell for putting on the finest show in the Northeast each year.

1972 CORN PALACE. The Tennessee Plowboy, Eddie Arnold, headlined the show. George McGovern's presidential campaign and the Vietnam War commanded the year's attention. "Relaxin' in South Dakota" echoed its theme through the decorative murals.

1973 CORN PALACE. Pat Boone, along with his family, was the star attraction. The annual redecorating job required about 3,000 bushels of corn, two ton of other grains and grasses, and about 175 pounds of nails. It costs the city approximately $15,000 to redecorate each year.

1973 PUTTING UP THE DOME. A 10-ton stucco dome was removed to be replaced by a new 4,200-pound yellow fiberglass dome that took central position. The dome arrived in pieces, which were put together by workmen from a New Brighton, Minnesota company. The new dome had a hatch in the back that allowed the flag to be run up the pole extending from the top of the dome.

1973 Pat Boone. Boone, a 1950s teen idol, was known as the "All American Boy." He recorded his biggest hits in the 1950s and 1960s and also made several movies. In later years, he entertained with his wife and daughters.

1974 Corn Palace. "The Founding Fathers" theme set the stage for Roy Rogers and Dale Evans, King and Queen of the West. They appeared in 15 performances. The palace had the fifth highest gross ticket sales in Corn Palace history. The decorators used brome grass for the first time along with sour dock to give a full look to the panels.

1974 MIDWAY. Nice 70-degree weather added to the midway's enjoyment.

1975 CORN PALACE. In anticipation of the country's 200th birthday, local artists, Don Durfee and Barbara Young, designed the Corn Palace in the spirit of 1776. The King Family, Alino Rey, The King Cousins, Bob Clarke, Kent Larsen, and the King Kiddies provided entertainment.

1975 KING FAMILY. The King family began in vaudeville in the 1920s with succeeding generations perpetuating their heritage of music. Hits of the family sold millions of records.

1976 BOB HOPE. Not only did Bob Hope entertain at the Corn Palace, he also participated in the Bob Hope Corn Palace Classic Golf Tournament in Mitchell. Hope was awarded an honorary doctors degree at Dakota Wesleyan. The Mitchell Veterans of Foreign Wars Post presented him with a plaque with these words, "to a man who has given so unselfishly of himself to entertain overseas military personnel." Ray Eppel, chairman of the Corn Palace Committee, also presented a plaque in appreciation of 14 performances in seven days.

1976 CORN PALACE. King of comedy, Bob Hope, appearing in 14 performances, said he came upon the recommendation of Lawrence Welk. Hope added much needed humor to a drought-stricken state.

1977 CORN PALACE. Red Skelton, internationally known clown comedian, and Roy Clark, a folk singer, shared the stage with Tanya Welk and the Keane Brothers. Various murals depicted ballet, drama, painting, Indian culture, and music, reflecting the theme "The Fine Arts."

1977 RED SKELTON. Skelton was known for his sketch comedy and his memorable characters, Freddie the Freeloader, Clem Kadiddlehopper, San Fernando Red, Junior the Mean Little Kid, and several others. He closed his television performances with these words. "I personally believe we were put here to build and not to destroy. So if by chance some day you're not feeling well and you should remember some silly little thing I've said or done and it brings back a smile to your face or a chuckle to your heart—then my purpose as your clown has been fulfilled. Goodnight and may God bless."

1978 CORN PALACE. The palace nearly shut down due to electrical problems. The theme South Dakota birds embellished the palace. Barbara Eden, Comedian Rich Little, Victor Borge, and the Christy Minstrel show entertained the crowds. Charles Kuralt was also in town.

1979 FIRE. On June 21, an arsonist set fire to the palace. The large minaret and two kiosks were lost in the blaze and had to be removed.

1979 FIRE. Water damages to the inside of the palace made repair costs skyrocket. Approximately one million dollars was spent on repairs. When repairs were completed, the palace had a new roof, security system, new lighting, and an automatic sprinkler system.

1979 DANNY DAVIS. Born in Maine, Davis started playing trumpet in a Catholic youth band. Davis and his eight-piece band traveled across rural American 265-280 days a year. "I really enjoy the clean air out here," he said.

1979 CORN PALACE. Repairs to the palace were completed in time for Corn Palace week. Jim Nabors of Gomer Pyle fame received a standing ovation at every performance. Danny Davis, the Nashville Brass, the Mill Brothers, magician Mark Wilson, Jerry Marad's Harmonicats, and John Shirley and his balloon tricks also performed.

Six

A TOUCH OF COUNTRY
1980–2000

1980 CORN PALACE. A country variety show starred Bill Anderson, Ferlin Husky, Archie Campbell, Serendipity Singers, Brenda Lee, Pat Paulsen, The Four Lads, Mulleague and Company, and Tinilau's Tahitians. The palace was absent its large center dome destroyed by fire a year earlier. The photo by Clyde Goin captures the theme "South Dakota Recreation."

1980 BILL ANDERSON. Anderson, a star of the famous Grand Ole Opry in Nashville, starred in his own weekly show for nine years. He has been honored as male vocalist of the year and songwriter of the year on three different occasions.

1980 PANEL. Made entirely of split ears of corn, this mural depicts two Indian symbols most important to their past existence, the buffalo—symbol of life, and the altar of corn. Calvin Schultz has designed the murals since 1976.

110

1981 Corn Palace. Tennessee Ernie Ford provided the main entertainment. The festival honored former palace designer and South Dakota Laureate Oscar Howe. Six panels, featuring original Howe designs, were dedicated. The city passed a controversial ordinance that allowed liquor sales in the Corn Palace for special occasions. Polka Mass was held for the first time.

1982 Corn Palace. Red Skelton brought laughter to crowds. Outside panels were not changed for the first time since 1945. Panels were selected from the 1948-1971 period when Howe was the designing artist.

111

1983 CORN PALACE. The *Daily Republic* reported that shrinkage problems had occurred this year since the moisture content of the corn was too high. B. J. Thomas performed as well as the Lennon Sisters who drew in 14,555 attendees during their four-day show.

1984 CORN PALACE. An article, published in *Old Fashioned Country Diary*, awarded the Corn Palace the distinction of being the world's largest bird feeder. Carol Lawrence was signed as well as other entertainers Roger Williams and Shelly West. The first day of Corn Palace was met with rain turning to snow.

112

1984 MIDWAY. Corn Palace visitors enjoy exploring the midway.

1985 CORN PALACE. Headliners included Bobby Vinton, Louis Anderson, Box Car Willie, Comedians Williams and Ree, and Country Time Jamboree. Playing for the Corn Polka Festival were accordionists Linda Lee Brown and Myron Floren.

1985 WILLIAMS AND REE. Also known as the Indian and the White Guy, Terry Ree and Bruce Williams have toured across the nation and appeared on the Nashville Network. Ree grew up in Pierre and Williams came from Mountain Home, Idaho. They met at Black Hills State College, Spearfish in 1968 where they began playing in a band. To take up the slack time, they added ad lib humor. They soon learned that comedy was where they excelled and proceeded to hone their skills. Since then, they have been entertaining audiences with their ethnic humor and poke-fun-at-everything style.

1986 Corn Palace

1986 CORN PALACE. In addition to the slate of entertainers, the festival sponsored Big Band dancing, the sixth annual Polka Festival, and a midway featuring shows and agricultural exhibits. Calvin Schultz designed panels for the theme "First Americans."

1986 TOM T. HALL. Hall made an appearance at the Corn Palace along with The Tennessee River Boys, Roger Miller, the gospel music of The Masters V, and the Hinsons.

1987 CORN PALACE. Calvin Schultz, a former art teacher, designed panels for the last ten years. He designed antique cars for this year's theme. In speaking of the process of designing panels, he said that designs must be practical. "The corn cobs don't allow for intricate shadings . . . you have to eliminate a lot of detail," he said. The Charlie Daniels Band, Doug Kershaw, Eddie Rabbitt and Sylvia, Christy Lane and the Masters V, and the seventh annual Polka Festival provided entertainment.

1988 CORN PALACE. Service symbols decorated the exterior of the palace. Larry Gatlin, Williams and Ree, Mickey Gilley, Kathy Mattea, and the Southern Gospel Concert, The Hemphills, entertained the crowds.

1988 KATHY MATTEA. Country singer Kathy Mattea has earned four top-ten country singles, a Grammy nomination, multiple Country Music Association and Music City News award nominations, and has performed in front of millions of fans.

1988 MICKEY GILLEY. To date, Gilley has landed 18 singles in the number one spot. In 1976, Gilley swept the ACM Awards. He was named Entertainer of the Year, Top Male Vocalist, and won Song of the Year, Single of the Year, and Album of the Year. He exhibits distinctive vocal talents as well as dexterous piano playing style.

1989 CRYSTAL GALE. Born the youngest of eight children in the coal-mining town of Paintsville, Kentucky, Gale's life was always filled with music. She has recorded many platinum selling albums and has appeared on a wide variety of television shows.

1989 CORN PALACE. Designs of the Corn Palace exterior remained the same. The interior of the building underwent a radical facelift, creating a more up-to-date, attractive look inside. The theme presented the last century in the state from 1889–1989. The entertainers included Crystal Gale, Mel Tillis, and Don Williams.

1989 PANEL. A mural depicted the state animal—the coyote, the state bird—the Chinese ring-necked pheasant, and the state flower—the pasque.

1990 CORN PALACE. Calvin Schultz designed this year's theme, "Celebrate the Century." It featured important moments in time since South Dakota became a state.

1990 PANEL. The postcard close up of four panels, designed by artist, Calvin Schultz, depicted South Dakota scenes since statehood to follow the theme "Celebrate the Century."

1990 OAK RIDGE BOYS. The top entertainers included Charley Pride, Oak Ridge Boys, Lionel Cartwright, Williams and Ree, and Janie Frickie. Rock 'n' Roll Night featured Bill Haley's Comets, the Drifters, and the Box Tops. Eddy Skeets and his orchestra provided Big Band music.

1991 CORN PALACE. "The Good Life" was this year's theme. The Corn Palace asked local artists to submit designs based upon their concept of the good life.

1991 PATTY LOVELESS.
Performers for the 1991 palace
included Patty Loveless, Lee
Greenwood, Suzy Bogguss,
Bellamy Brothers, Ronnie Milsap,
and the Forrester Sisters. Sha Na
Na entertained during Rock 'n'
Roll Night.

1992 CORN PALACE. Tammy Wynette, Oak Ridge Boys, Tanya Tucker, Shari Lewis, Myron
Floren, and stars of the Lawrence Welk show entertained the audiences.

1992 PANEL. A worker carefully fills in the coding on the sketched outline on roofing paper, much like a paint-by-numbers project.

1993 CORN PALACE. Decorations from the previous palace were carried over to the 1993 Corn Palace. A South Dakota theme predominated.

1993 MARK CHESTNUT. Myron Floren, Williams and Ree, Marty Stuart, Kathy Mattea, and Mark Chestnut performed at the 101st Corn Palace. The 13th annual Polka Festival also offered entertainment to the polka fans.

1994 CORN PALACE. Calvin Schultz designed the panels with the theme "Myths, Legends and Fables." Clyde Goin took the Corn Palace photo.

1994 TRISHA YEARWOOD.
The palace provided an array of
entertainment with the appearances
of Baker Street Music for Kids, The
Cathedrals gospel group, Sammy
Kershaw, Trisha Yearwood, Kris
Kuester, Ralna English, Bobby
Burgess and Elaine Balden, Tom
Netherton, Smothers Brothers, and
Shawn Camp.

1995 CORN PALACE. Calvin Schultz designed the panels to commemorate the Corn Palace
stampede rodeo during its 25th year. The photo was taken by Marvin L. Stavig.

1995 DIAMOND RIO. Diamond Rio, Hal Ketchum, Three Dog Night, The Cathedrals, and Dwain Muller and his orchestra gave performances. Country music concerts lost money. Organizers considered reducing the number of entertainers the following year. Committee members felt that part of the problem was due to the fact that most singers limited their performances to one show and to the continuing cost of entertainment.

1996 CORN PALACE. Calvin Schultz drew from his own past and came up with designs for the country school, country church, and spring calving for the "Memories" motif. The Army Ground Forces Jazz and Dixeland Bands, Joe Diffie, Myron Floren, and stars from the Lawrence Welk brought enjoyment to the audiences.

126

1997 CORN PALACE. Myron appeared on stage for the sixth straight year. The Village People, Glad, and Blackhawk also appeared. Panels reflected a "Hunt South Dakota" theme.

1998 CORN PALACE. "Building a Nation" was the theme for the year. Frankie Valli and the Four Seasons appeared the first night with Hondo the Magician as their opener. Williams and Ree and The Nitty Gritty Dirt Band performed the following evening. Martina McBride, Theea Daniels, Myron Floren, Arthur Duncan, Bobby and Elaine, and Ralna English also entertained. Gospel night starred a local Deb Weitala. Five bands played for the 18th annual Polka Fest.

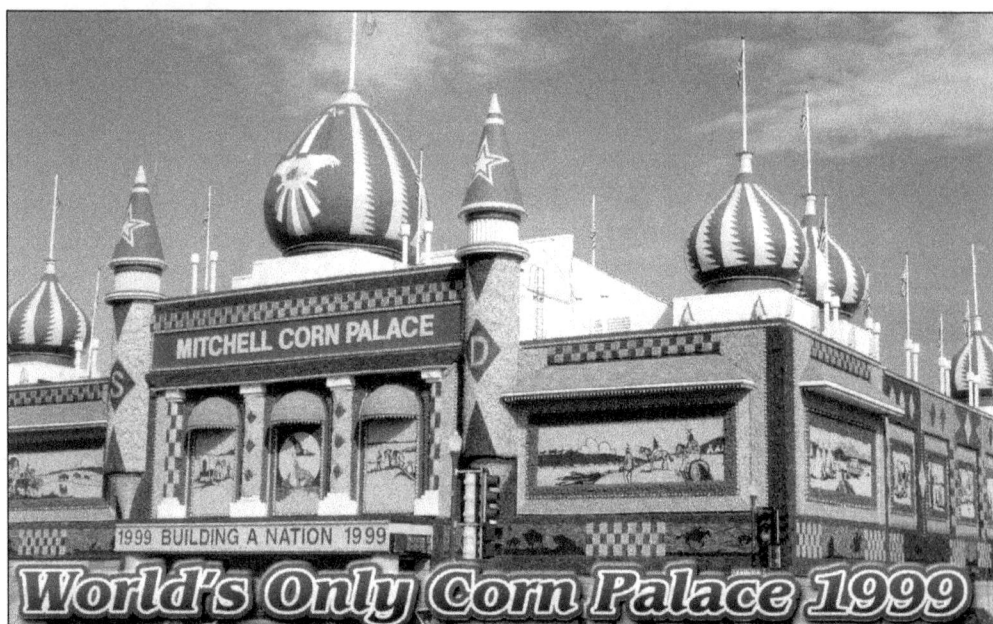

1999 CORN PALACE. The 38 Special, Ozark Mountain Daredevils, and Jim Nabors made appearances at the palace. Other events included a cowboy poetry round up, Corn Tucky Derby Races, a corn eating contest, and gospel music.

2000 CORN PALACE. The palace ushered in the new millennium, secure in its spirit of tradition. Panels were decorated with scenes from the past. Weather played havoc with the palace this year. Snow and wind damaged domes and minarets. Repairmen discovered that the wooden platforms for both minarets had decayed over time, probably causing the damage. Performers included Wayne Newton, Kenny Chesney, Gwen Matthews, and Britney Spears.

Visit us at
arcadiapublishing.com